Sports Fun!

Tennis

by Rachael Barnes

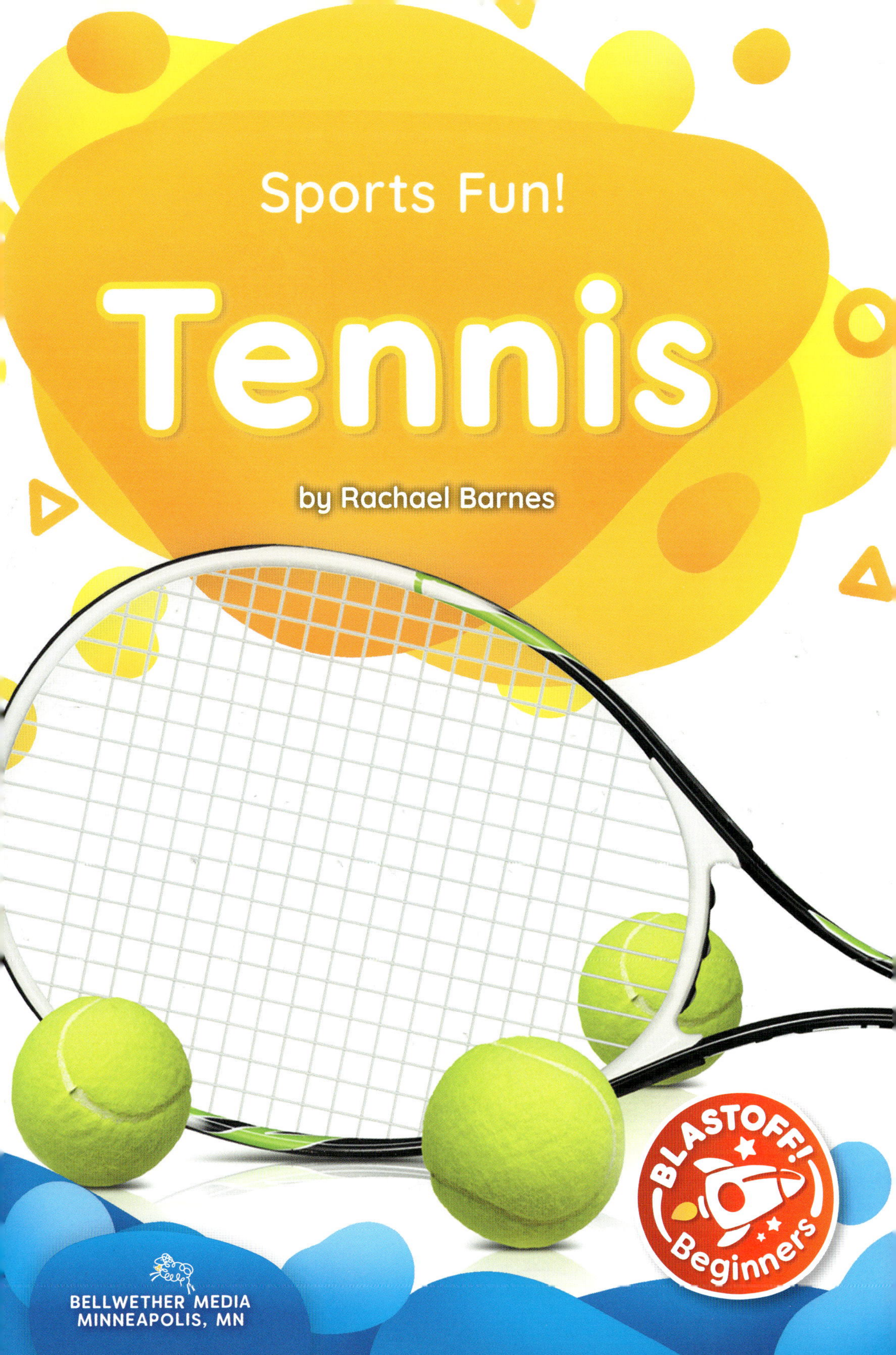

BELLWETHER MEDIA
MINNEAPOLIS, MN

Blastoff! Beginners are developed by literacy experts and educators to meet the needs of early readers. These engaging informational texts support young children as they begin reading about their world. Through simple language and high frequency words paired with crisp, colorful photos, Blastoff! Beginners launch young readers into the universe of independent reading.

Sight Words in This Book

come	many	play	use
for	on	the	we
have	one	they	
here	or	this	
in	other	time	
it	people	to	

This edition first published in 2024 by Bellwether Media, Inc.

Library of Congress Cataloging-in-Publication Data

Names: Barnes, Rachael, author.
Title: Tennis / by Rachael Barnes.
Description: Minneapolis, MN : Bellwether Media, 2024. | Series: Blastoff! beginners. Sports fun! | Includes bibliographical references and index. | Audience: Ages 4-7 | Audience: Grades K-1
Identifiers: LCCN 2023035140 (print) | LCCN 2023035141 (ebook) | ISBN 9798886877700 (library binding) | ISBN 9798886878646 (ebook)
Subjects: LCSH: Tennis--Juvenile literature.
Classification: LCC GV996.5 .B34 2024 (print) | LCC GV996.5 (ebook) | DDC 796.342--dc23/eng/20230804
LC record available at https://lccn.loc.gov/2023035140
LC ebook record available at https://lccn.loc.gov/2023035141

Editor: Kieran Downs Designer: Gabriel Hilger

Printed in the United States of America, North Mankato, MN.

Table of Contents

Match Day!

Time for
the **match**.
We love tennis!

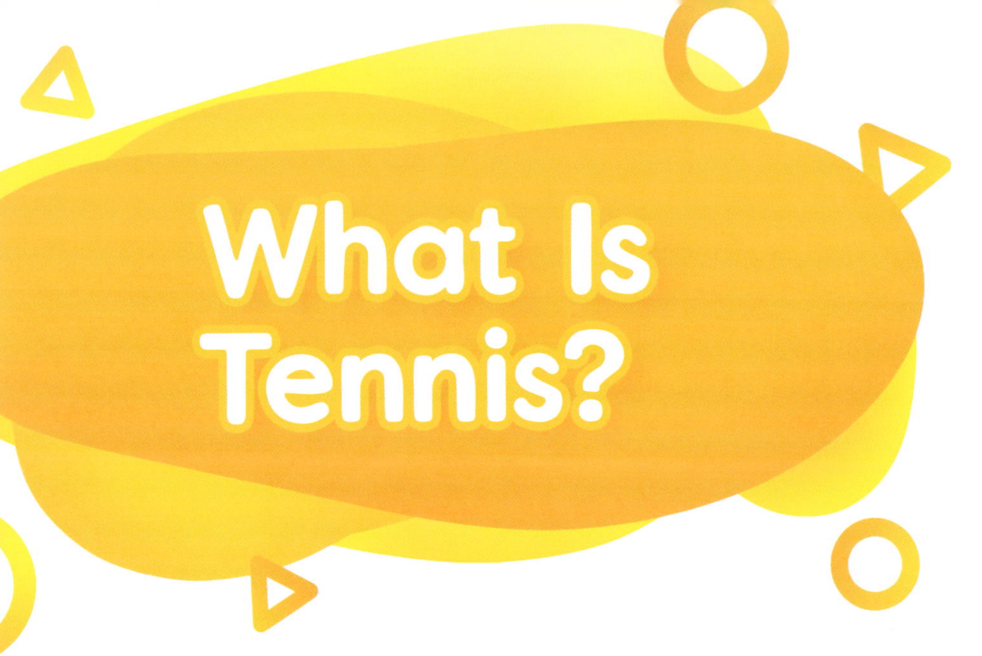

What Is Tennis?

People play tennis on **courts**. Players play alone or in pairs.

court

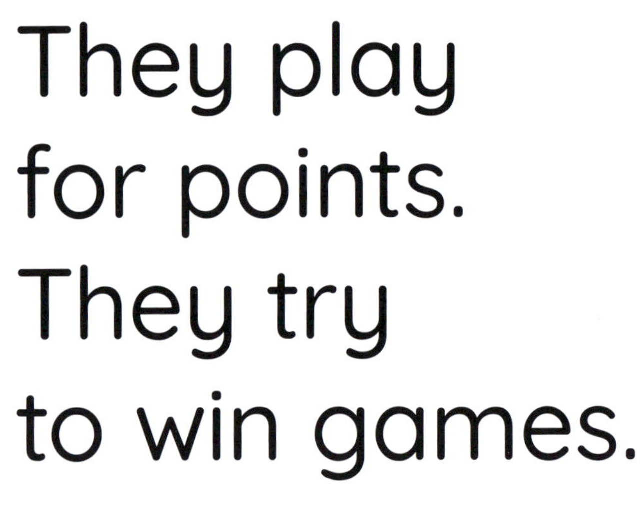

They play
for points.
They try
to win games.

Matches have many games.

On the Court

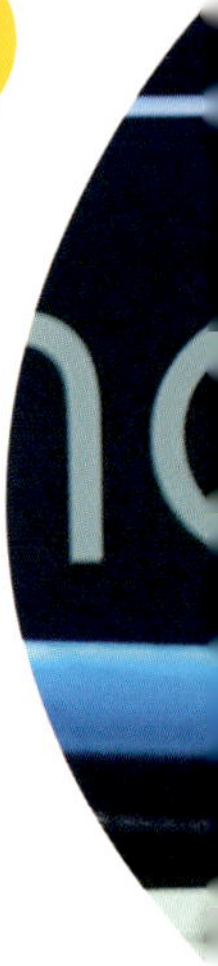

Players hit the ball
over the net.
They use **rackets**.

racket

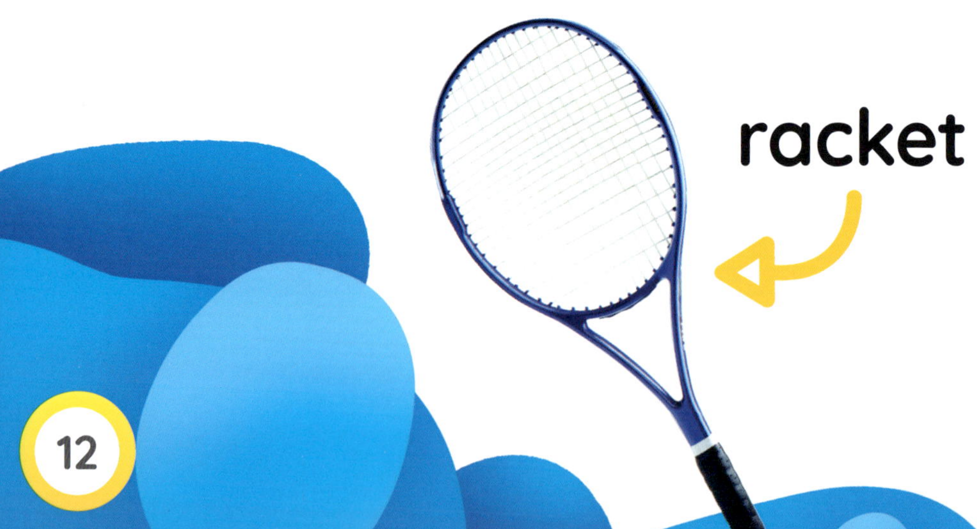

net

One player starts the point. They **serve**.

serving

The other player hits the ball back.

This player missed. The other player wins the point!

Here comes
the ball. This player
gives it spin. Point!

Tennis Facts

Playing Tennis

Tennis Moves

serve

hit the ball

spin the ball

Glossary

courts

places to play tennis

match

a group of tennis games

rackets

tools used to hit tennis balls

serve

to hit the ball to start a point

To Learn More

ON THE WEB

FACTSURFER

Factsurfer.com gives you a safe, fun way to find more information.

1. Go to www.factsurfer.com.
2. Enter "tennis" into the search box and click .
3. Select your book cover to see a list of related content.

Index

The images in this book are reproduced through the courtesy of: Chones, front cover, p. 1; Pixel-Shot, p. 3; Patrick Foto, p. 4; FamVeld, pp. 4-5; Guy Cowdry, pp. 6-7; Dianne Avery Photography/ Getty Images, pp. 8-9; SolStock, pp. 10-11, 22 (hit the ball); pukach, p. 12; Manuela Davies/ AP Images, pp. 12-13; Master1305, p. 14; ptaxa, pp. 14-15; Dustin Satloff/ AP Images, pp. 16-17; New Africa, p. 18; pixdeluxe, pp. 18-19; Ulrike Schmitt-Hartmann/ Getty Images, pp. 20-21; LPETTET, p. 22 (playing tennis); Anna Sadovskaia, p. 22 (serve); Elkhophoto, p. 22 (spin the ball); Formatoriginal, p. 23 (courts); martinedoucet, p. 23 (match); Olena Yakobchuk, p. 23 (rackets); mgstudyo, p. 23 (serve).